Counting in the Rain Forest 1-2-3

Aaron R. Murray

Enslow Elementary

an imprint of

Enslow Publishers, Inc.

40 Industrial Road
Box 398
Berkeley Heights, NJ 07922
USA

http://www.enslow.com

Enslow Elementary, an imprint of Enslow Publishers, Inc.
Enslow Elementary® is a registered trademark of Enslow Publishers, Inc.

Library of Congress Cataloging-in-Publication Data

Murray, Aaron R.
  Counting in the rain forest 1-2-3 / Aaron R. Murray.
     p. cm. — (All about counting in the biomes)
  Includes index.
  Summary: "Introduces pre-readers to simple concepts about the rain forest using short sentences and
repetition"—Provided by publisher.
  ISBN 978-0-7660-4055-7
  1. Rain forest ecology—Juvenile literature. 2. Rain forests—Juvenile literature. 3. Counting—Juvenile
literature. I. Title. II. Title: Counting in the rain forest one-two-three.
  QH541.5.R27M857 2012
  577.34—dc23
                              2011039557
Future editions:
Paperback ISBN 978-1-4644-0063-6
ePUB ISBN 978-1-4645-0970-4
PDF ISBN 978-1-4646-0970-1

Printed in the United States of America
032012 Lake Book Manufacturing, Inc., Melrose Park, IL
10 9 8 7 6 5 4 3 2 1

To Our Readers: We have done our best to make sure all Internet Addresses in this book were active and
appropriate when we went to press. However, the author and the publisher have no control over and assume no
liability for the material available on those Internet sites or on other Web sites they may link to. Any comments
or suggestions can be sent by e-mail to comments@enslow.com or to the address on the back cover.

✿ Enslow Publishers, Inc., is committed to printing our books on recycled paper. The paper in every book
contains 10% to 30% post-consumer waste (PCW). The cover board on the outside of each book contains
100% PCW. Our goal is to do our part to help young people and the environment too!

Photo Credits: © 2011 Photos.com, a division of Getty Images, pp. 4, 20; iStockphoto.com: © Dominic
DeGrazier, p. 18; © Jeff Hathaway, p. 14; Photos.com: Edward White, p. 12, Joel Peters, p. 16, John Gyovai,
p. 3 petal), Jupiterimages, p. 10; Shutterstock.com, pp. 1, 3 (frog, water lily), 6, 8, 22.
Cover Photo: Shutterstock.com

Note to Parents and Teachers

Help pre-readers get a jump start on reading. These lively stories introduce simple concepts with repetition
of words and short simple sentences. Photos and illustrations fill the pages with color and effectively
enhance the text. Free Educator Guides are available for this series at www.enslow.com. Search for the
All About Counting in the Biomes series name.

Contents

Words to Know

frog   **petals**   **water lily**

Poison
dart frog

Let's count!

1

One frog

Chameleon

Two eyes

Three-toed
sloth

Three toes

Four birds

Macaques

Five monkeys

Six petals

Seven bats

Rain forest
spider

Eight legs

Giant water lilies

Nine water lilies

Komodo
dragon

Ten claws

Read More

Amstutz, Lisa Jo. *Rain Forest Animal Adaptations.* Mankato, Minn.: Capstone, 2011.

Gordon, Sharon. *Rain Forest Animals.* Tarrytown, N.Y.: Benchmark Books, 2008.

Serafini, Frank. *Looking Closely in the Rain Forest.* Tonawanda, N.Y.: Kids Can Press, 2010.

Web Sites

National Geographic Kids: Tropical Rain Forests
   <http://kids.nationalgeographic.com/kids/photos/tropical-rainforests/>
Rainforest Alliance: Kids' Corner
   <http://www.rainforest-alliance.org/kids>

Index

Guided Reading Level: A
Guided Reading Leveling System is based on the guidelines recommended by Fountas and Pinnell.

Word Count: 23